the Hero Field Guide

Volume 2

Written by Matt Langdon
Illustrated by Matthew Osmon

"You are lucky in life if you have the right heroes. I advise all of you, to the extent you can, to pick out a few heroes."
— Warren Buffett

We created this book for our daughters. As they grow up they are going to need some heroes. As their dads, we can provide our example, our heroes, and our hopes. But we know they need more. They need heroes to be inspired by, to emulate, and to share. We want them to have heroes of all shapes and sizes, colors and ages, nationalities and genders.

And we want this for you and your kids too.

So here it is - the second field guide of heroes to help your children (and ours) get started creating their own collection of personal heroes.

Matt & Matt

Matt Langdon has been helping kids become heroes since 1994. He lives in Australia with his wife and daughter and kangaroos and wombats. He loves discovering new heroes and eating good chocolate.

Matthew Osmon has been creating caricatures since high school when he used to draw his teachers and chapel speakers. He lives in Flint, Michigan with his wife and daughter. When he isn't teaching art to his high school students, he is doing his best to create it.

If you would like to suggest a hero for the next volume, please visit
herofieldguides.com.

Dedicated to Ada and Vienna

Mridula Sarabhai

Mridula was born into the prominent Sarabhai family in India. As a child she became interested in the work of Mohandas Gandhi, who was attempting to free India of British colonial rule. When she was ten she joined a children's group called the Monkey Army. This group followed the leadership of Gandhi, refusing to wear clothes or buy items made by the British. Her early activities continued into adulthood when she became a politician. She worked in women's rights and became very popular. She was also known for her "boy-cut" hair and masculine clothing.

On the 15th of August 1947, the British Empire of India was split in two, creating the separate nations of India and Pakistan. Pakistan became the home of Muslims while India was primarily for the Hindus and Sikhs. This separation meant over ten million people had to move their homes to a new country. More than half a million people died in riots and religious violence. Mridula began a peace mission, helping both sides of the conflict. She helped refugees escape and cared for incoming migrating families. Leaders from both sides praised her efforts.

"I felt honoured that I had been entrusted with this difficult and responsible job."

Mridula Sarabhai 1911-1974

Fred Korematsu

Fred was born in California to Japanese immigrant parents. While he was working as a welder, Japan bombed Pearl Harbor and thrust the United States into war. Soon after the attack, Fred was fired from his job and very quickly found it impossible to find work in a suddenly racist city. In early 1942, it became illegal for Japanese people to live anywhere near the West Coast due to fears that they were signalling information to Japanese submarines. Over 100,000 Japanese-Americans were sent to internment camps. Fred refused to go and had plastic surgery on his eyelids in the hope he would appear to be Spanish or Hawaiian. It didn't work and he was arrested. He was sent to a prison camp in Utah where he worked eight hours a day and lived in a horse stall.

With the help of a lawyer, Fred took his case to the Supreme Court and lost. Forty years later, that decision was found to be based on lies and Fred was pardoned. Fred remained an activist throughout his life, and in 1998 he received the Presidential Medal of Freedom. After the attacks of September 11th he urged lawmakers to remember the illegality of locking people up simply because they looked like those who had attacked the United States.

"If you have the feeling that something is wrong, don't be afraid to speak up."

Fred Korematsu 1919 - 2005

Amelia Earhart

Amelia was six years old when the first airplane completed a successful flight. At ten, she saw her first plane up close at a State Fair. She was not very impressed. However, when she was twenty-four, she fell in love with flying after going on a ten-minute flight, and she started taking lessons. Six months later she purchased her own plane and called it Canary. A year later she had set a world record for altitude for a female flyer. She never looked back.

In 1928, Amelia became the first woman to travel across the Atlantic Ocean in a plane. She did none of the flying, but she couldn't stop thinking about doing it alone some day. That flight made her famous, and she became a leader in aviation and women's rights in the United States. She helped form the Ninety-Nines, a group dedicated to promoting and supporting female pilots.

Amelia realized her dream when she became the second person to fly solo nonstop across the Atlantic in 1932. She achieved numerous distance and speed records over the years and finally decided she wanted to be the first person to fly all the way around the world. That attempt was her last, as she and her crew disappeared over the Pacific in 1932, presumed dead.

"Never interrupt someone doing what you said couldn't be done."

Amelia Earhart 1897-1937

Erin Brockovich

Erin grew up with dyslexia and fought through it with the "stick-to-it-iveness" promoted by her mother. This attitude found her an office job at a law firm after a car accident left her struggling for money. While working in that job she came across a set of records showing a group of families suffering from regular nosebleeds, headaches, and tiredness. She suspected that there might be a problem with the drinking water of these families.

She discovered that the groundwater had been contaminated for decades by a large and powerful energy company. Erin and her boss decided to go to court for these families. For numerous years they battled in the courts, dealt with intimidation, and finally came out as winners in one of the biggest court decisions in history. The families were paid and Erin went on to represent other families all over the world in their fights against corporate poisoning. Her "stick-to-it-iveness" now helps people overcome the problems facing them.

"If you follow your heart, if you listen to your gut, and if you extend your hand to help another, not for any agenda, but for the sake of humanity, you are going to find the truth."

Ceasar Chavez

Cesar was born into a poor farming family in Arizona. When his father got into crippling debt, the family moved to California to work as migrant farmers. Cesar stopped going to school in seventh grade to help make money for the family by picking crops full time. This work made him aware of the terrible conditions that so many migrant workers experienced. He realized the way to help was not through charity, but by organizing the thousands of workers. Alone they were weak, but together they were strong.

He began urging migrant workers to register to vote, and he planned marches and other protests. In 1962, he created the National Farm Workers Association with Dolores Huerta. Nonviolence became an important feature of his efforts at this time. Cesar believed peaceful protest was the only way for long term success. His five decades of campaigning changed the lives of farmers in the United States forever. He is remembered as a champion of human rights and also the rights of animals - he spent the last twenty-five years of life as a vegetarian.

*"Non-violence is not inaction.
It is not discussion. It is not for the timid or weak...
Non-violence is hard work."*

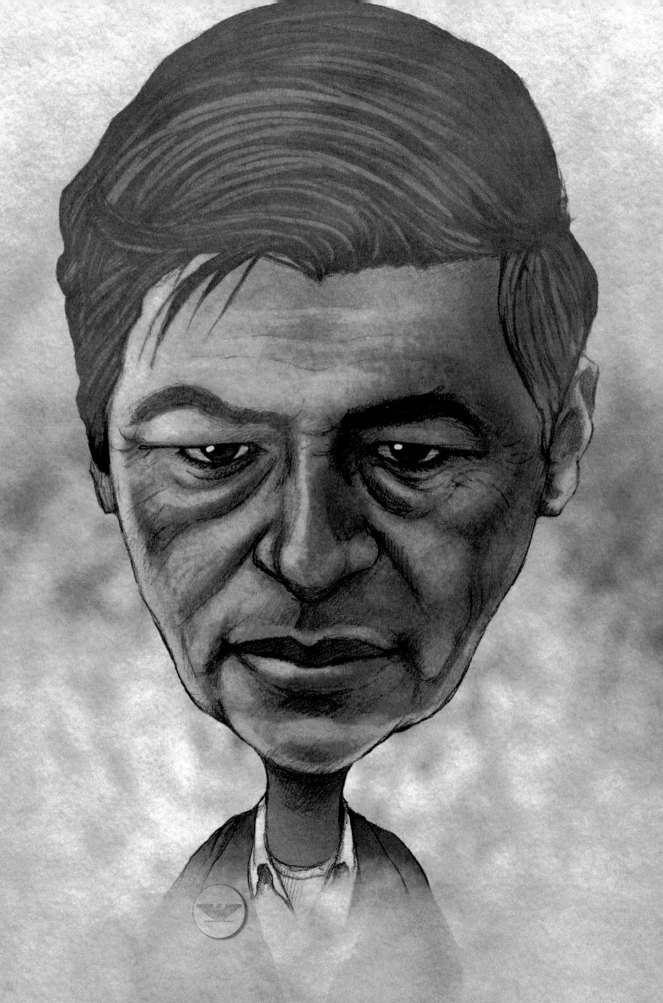

Ceasar Chavez 1927 - 1993

Harriet Tubman

As a teenaged slave in Maryland, Harriet had her head smashed by a metal weight. She was sure the only reason she survived was that her hair, which had never been brushed, took most of the impact. The injury gave her headaches, seizures, and visions for the rest of her life. A life of beatings and punishment made her long for freedom, and one day she finally ran away. She headed north, guided by the North Star and with the help of the Underground Railroad network of supporters.

Not content with her own freedom, Harriet went back to rescue her family and friends over the course of three trips. Her success at remaining uncaptured on these dangerous missions encouraged her to go back again and again. The tricks she used on her journeys have become legendary. She brought around seventy people to safety over eight years and gained the nickname of "Moses". In thirteen trips, she "never lost a passenger" and she was never captured.

"Every great dream begins with a dreamer."

Harriet Tubman 1822 - 1913

Kathryn Bolkovac

Kathryn was a police officer in Lincoln, Nebraska specializing in crimes against women and children. In 1999 she accepted a new job with a private government contractor to work for the United Nations International Police Task Force in post-war Bosnia. As a single mom, Kathryn saw this as a great opportunity to use her police training and skills at the international level. She would be able to train local Bosnian police and promote democratic principles. This job paid very well for a short period of time so this could also help Kathryn pay for the college education of her children.

When she arrived in Bosnia she quickly became aware that some of the law enforcers and international aid workers within the United Nations system were also breaking the law. She discovered a large sex slave operation being run and used by members of the international forces. Kathryn spent almost two years in Bosnia investigating and making official reports to UN officials. Her complaints and work were ignored and covered up by both the United Nations managment and the private government contractor. She was eventuallly unlawfully fired and was forced to take her case to British court. She won her case in 2003 and has campaigned ever since to expose the injustices that occurred in Bosnia and continue to occur in mission areas around the world.

Her work in exposing these issues worldwide while denouncing the growing use of private contractors being used in military and police functions led to her 2015 nomination of the Nobel Peace Prize.

"I do the best I can, I work hard, and hope that one day things will change."

Lawrence Oates

Lawrence led an active life enjoying hunting, sports, and his time in the British Army. He fought in the Boer War in South Africa, where he became known for his courage and selflessness - as well as a self-effacing sense of humor. During the war his left leg was shattered by a gunshot. Surgery left the leg one inch shorter and created a limp, but it didn't slow him down.

In 1911, Lawrence joined Robert Scott's team in the race to be the first to reach the South Pole. His expertise with animals led him to manage the nineteen ponies who were key to the success of the mission. When he, Scott, and three others finally made it to the pole, they found that Roald Amundsen had beaten them. The disappointed group started heading back to the main group, but it was slow going. Lawrence had been hiding the fact that his feet were frostbitten and the cold was creating excruciating pain in his old wound. He knew his party would die if they kept waiting for him, so he asked them to leave him in his sleeping bag to die. They refused. The next morning he left the tent and said, "I am just going outside and may be some time." He died shortly after.

"I am just going outside and may be some time."

Lawrence Oates 1880 - 1912

Léo Major

When Canada declared war on Germany in World War II, Léo joined the army. He wanted to prove to his father that he was somebody to be proud of. Within a couple of days of landing at Normandy on D Day he lost an eye after his first encounter with an SS group. He refused to be evacuated and continued fighting in numerous battles. In one battle, he captured ninety-three soldiers by himself and marched them back to Canadian troops.

One night, Léo and his friend, Willy, went to investigate the German capabilities in a Dutch town called Zwolle. The buddies decided to take over the town instead. Willie was killed at around midnight, forcing Léo into a rage. He ran into the city making as much noise as he could, shooting off his gun, throwing grenades, and lighting buildings on fire. A garrison of hundreds of Germans fled, thinking the entire Canadian army was entering the city. For this he received a Distinguished Conduct Medal. He won a second for bravery in the Korean War. The city of Zwolle remembers his rescue every year.

"If I am a hero then I am a hero.
I did what I did because I had to do it."

Temar Boggs

Temar was fifteen years old when he and his friend heard about an abduction in their neighborhood. A five year old girl had been snatched, and people had started spreading the word to look out for her. Temar and his friend, Chris, decided to form their own search party and began patrolling the streets, woods, and local creek. The group of friends didn't find anything and returned home to find dozens of firefighters, police officers, and neighbors swarming the streets. Temar and Chris chose to go back out again, this time on bikes.

Temar spotted a car make a sudden turn away from a police road block and decided to follow it. He got close enough to notice the young girl in the passenger seat. Rather than turn back and risk losing the car in the maze-like streets of the subdivision, he followed it. After a short time, the car stopped and the side door opened, letting the girl escape. She ran to Temar and he grabbed her in his arms. With the girl on his shoulders, he rode back to her home, giving her up to a firefighter.

"I'm just a normal person who did a thing that anybody else would do."

Temar Boggs 1998 - Present

When France was defeated in World War II she was living with her husband in southern France, and she started working with the French Resistance. She helped by delivering messages, packages, and, eventually, escaped Allied prisoners. Her exploits became well known among the Germans, earning her the nickname "White Mouse" and a place at the top of the most wanted list. Nancy fled France when it became clear she would be caught. In Britain, she was trained by a secret spy organization and returned to work in France, leading resistance fighters against German troops. She was a bold warrior and regularly surprised those she fought with and against. After the war many countries presented her with medals which she sold to make sure the rest of her life was comfortable. She was never sentimental.

"I hate wars and violence but if they come then I don't see why we women should just wave our men a proud goodbye and then knit them balaclavas."

Mary Seacole

Mary loved mimicking her mother, who was a healer in Jamaica. While watching her mother with patients, Mary would practice on her dolls and sometimes her pets. Eventually she was allowed to help with the human patients and became a healer in her own right. Mary loved traveling and was known for her nursing ability when epidemics like cholera or yellow fever appeared.

On one of her numerous visits to London she became aware of the lack of proper care for soldiers in the Crimean War. Mary immediately applied to be sent to war as a nurse, but was refused. She worried that it was because of the color of her skin, so she found a way to pay for herself to travel to the battle zone. Once there, she was horrified by the conditions and set up a ramshackle building dubbed the British Hotel. The building provided food and shelter to those who needed it, and Mary often went directly to the front, risking being shot, to nurse wounded soldiers. She left the war virtually bankrupt, but she is remembered fondly as someone who made an enormous difference to everyone involved in the war.

"And as often as the bad news came,
I thought it my duty to ride up to the hut and do my woman's work."

Mary Seacole 1805 - 1881

Pablo Picasso

Pablo is one of the most famous and important artists in modern times. Born in Spain, he spent much of his adult life in France. He was living in Paris at the beginning of World War II. Rather than flee from the invading German army, Picasso stayed in his adopted city despite pleas from numerous foreign governments. His fame protected him, but life changed dramatically, and he was never guaranteed safety. He was kicked out of his apartment and a number of friends were killed in concentration camps and other while fighting against the occupation.

The German secret police harassed him frequently and he was banned from exhibiting art - the Nazis considered his work degenerate. His famous painting, "Guernica", was his first major political statement against the fascist governments in Spain and Germany. When bronze sculpting was outlawed, Pablo continued, using smuggled bronze supplied by the French Resistance. His courage inspired artists of all kinds around him because they knew that at any minute, Pablo could have lost everything.

"When you have something to say, to express, any submission becomes unbearable in the long run."

Pablo Picasso 1881 - 1973

Shada Nasser

Shada was the first female lawyer in the largest city in Yemen, Sana'a. She was also the first woman in all of Yemen to work in a court with her face unveiled. Some judges and colleagues were supportive, but most were not. In one case she was asked to sit in the second row because the first row was reserved for men. She persevered through the challenges because she saw much injustice in Yemen, including the uninvestigated death of her father.

In 2006, Shada heard a commotion in the courthouse. A ten-year old girl had caught a taxi to the court and asked for a divorce from her thirty-year old husband. Child brides are common in Yemen, but this girl's husband had abused her so badly that she bravely risked trying to end the marriage, something virtually unheard of. Shada took on Nujood Ali's case for free after everyone else declined. Within two weeks, they had won the case. Nujood Ali went back home to play with her siblings, and Shada went on to fight for child brides across the country.

"This is my job. My job is very difficult.
But this is how I am, and I'll be like this forever."

Rigoberta Menchú

Rigoberta was born into a peasant family in the mountains of Guatemala. Her family were indigenous K'iche' people, related to the ancient Mayans. For the first thirty-seven years of her life Guatemala was engulfed in a civil war in which mostly native peoples were fighting against the government put in place by the United States. Rigoberta spent years after leaving school fighting for human rights in the face of death squads and the torture of rebels. When she was twenty-three, Rigoberta was forced to flee to Mexico.

From exile, she continued working to support the rights of the indigenous people. Any time she tried to return home she received death threats. After the war finally ended, she was able to convince Spanish courts to convict a number of the former military rulers. In 1992, she was awarded the Nobel Peace Prize for her work, and the fame allowed her to help with the struggles of other minority groups around the world.

"I am like a drop of water on a rock. After drip, drip, dripping in the same place, I begin to leave a mark, and I leave my mark in many people's hearts."

Rigoberta Menchú 1959 – Present

Nicholas Winton

After finishing school in England, Nicholas (or Nicky as he was known) spent many years working in Europe and practicing competitive fencing. He had been aware of the growing Nazi Party in Germany and thus gave up a vacation in Switzerland to help a friend work with Jewish refugees in Czechoslovakia. They were being forced out by the German invasion. Nicky immediately saw that hundreds of families were desperate to protect their children. He set up an office in the lobby of his hotel and started working on a solution.

Nicky established a train system to take children away from the danger to the relative safety of Britain. He tried to get other countries to accept children, but failed. The trains safely transported 669 children before all trains were cut off following the invasion of Poland. Nicky kept his work mostly secret for forty years until his wife discovered the books of children's photos in their attic. He died exactly seventy-six years after the largest train escape left Prague Station.

"Some people revel in taking risks, and some go through life taking no risks at all."

Nicholas Winton 1909 - 2015

Steve Biko

Steve was born in South Africa during the Apartheid era, in which the white minority kept black citizens separate and inferior. While studying medicine at university, he became active in student protests. He insisted that black students stop hoping that the problems of Apartheid would be solved by white people changing their minds and instead start working for a nonviolent solution themselves. This idea spread quickly and widely.

In five years he had become so influential that the government banned him from speaking or writing publicly. It was also forbidden to quote him. The banning included a restriction on movement, meaning he had to stay in town at all times. Despite these barriers, Steve worked tirelessly in a small office. He helped create centers for health and child care, a program to help the families of political prisoners, and a trust to help young people go to university. He was frequently detained, harassed, and arrested during this time. His final arrest resulted in a police beating so severe that he died in a jail cell, aged thirty.

"It is better to die for an idea that will live,
than to live for an idea that will die"

Steve Biko 1946 - 1977

Made in the USA
Middletown, DE
19 January 2016